AF483215

ISBN 13: 979-3-303778-2-4
LCCN: 2024913630

Illustrations and Design by Taillefer Long
create@illuminatedstories.org

Dedication

Dedicated to Clara Adams-Ender, the driving force behind Clara Cares. This book is a tribute to you. Your dedication and passion for helping others will never be forgotten. Your hard work has saved countless lives and inspired many others. We are proud to dedicate this book to you.

Quote

> "The foundation of every human relationship involves caring about oneself and others."

— Clara Adams-Ender, General Retired, MSN, RN

Table of Contents

ACKNOWLEDGEMENTS

To Ms. Lawanda Warthen, Vice President of Marketing and Chief of Staff at With Essential Means LLC (WEM), I extend my deepest gratitude for your generous contributions throughout this journey. Behind every successful writer is a guiding force, and you have been the steadfast presence keeping this project on course. Your support has maintained our direction and enabled me to share this story, inspire others, and make a meaningful impact. Your invaluable assistance has been a cornerstone in my continued writing pursuit. Thank you, Lawanda.

To my illustrator, Mr. Taillefer Long, for capturing my stories so beautifully and making the characters come alive. It's also impossible to express my gratitude to you for your unselfish understanding. Your hard work and dedication have been invaluable, and I am truly grateful for your contribution. You truly made my book a success and I am deeply thankful for all you have done. Thank you, Taillefer.

To Mr. James Byers, my proofreader and friend, has played a crucial role in improving the quality of my writing. His keen eye for detail and expertise in grammar and punctuation have significantly enhanced the clarity and coherence of my book. Without his meticulous review and insightful suggestions, my work would not have reached its full potential. I am immensely grateful for his valuable contributions and unwavering support throughout this writing journey. Thank you, James.

Finally, I want to express my profound gratitude to all who have joined me on this journey. Your unwavering support and belief in my ability to write this book are invaluable. I am immensely thankful for the remarkable individuals in my life and recognize that this accomplishment would not have been possible without each one of you.

The author,

Warren E. Morris

Prologue

Here is a heartwarming short story about a determined little girl who aspired to make a difference. This story takes place in a small town named Willow Springs, just outside of Raleigh, North Carolina nestled among rolling hills, beautiful trees, and farmland with tobacco fields as far as the eyes can see, there lived a little girl named Clara.

A gleam of wonder and curiosity glowed in Clara's large brown eyes. The thick, curly chestnut brown hair cascaded down her shoulders. The rich shade of her skin complemented the roundness and softness of her cheeks. A small, button-like nose adorned her face, and her cheeks were dotted with dimples when she smiled showing off her pearly white teeth.

Even at the youthful age of seven, Clara had a vivid imagination that was beyond her years. It was her lifelong goal to become successful, travel the world, and make a significant contribution to society.

Although Clara had a reasonable chance of achieving her goals, she was at a disadvantage due to the great odds that were stacked heavily against her. As the daughter of a sharecropper, the road to success would be challenging and limited for a girl from a poor family.

Although Clara faced many obstacles in her quest to achieve her dreams, her determination and willpower enabled her to overcome these obstacles and surpass her own expectations.

Her dream would indeed come true; she would become a leader, an independent thinker, a college graduate, a wife, a mother, a nurse and above all, a General in the United States Army.

CHAPTER 1

INTRODUCTION

This tale unfolds around Clara Leach, a girl who defies numerous challenges to emerge as a beacon of positivity. "Clara Cares" encapsulates the essence of confronting adversities and triumphing over them. It is a narrative that highlights how belief, perseverance, and compassion pave the way to achievement. Clara discovers that she can overcome any obstacle and make a positive difference in the world. Her story will inspire many.

Clara's odyssey is a powerful beacon, proving that no challenge is insurmountable. Her narrative celebrates the strength of bravery and tenacity. It is an inspiring call to action, echoing with hope and vigor, that encourages readers to pursue the greatest versions of themselves. Clara's story resonates with people of all ages, backgrounds, and circumstances, and serves as a reminder of the power we have within to never give up. It is a story that will motivate and inspire you to reach your fullest potential.

The difficulties she encountered as a sharecropper's daughter shaped her into the compassionate individual she is now. Clara's story is a testament to the power of perseverance and never giving up on your dreams. It is a reminder of the importance of believing in yourself and of never letting any obstacle stand in the way of success. It is a message of hope and a source of inspiration for future generations.

Clara was born and raised in Willow Springs, North Carolina, alongside her nine siblings: four brothers and five sisters. As the fourth child in a nurturing family, she was always eager to contribute.

Clara was inspired by her siblings to tackle challenging tasks, and she was always ready to lend a hand. She consistently volunteered first for any assignment. From her early years, she developed a strong sense of independence and resilience.

These valuable life lessons fostered in Clara a deep appreciation for the virtues of teamwork and determination. Overall, Clara's childhood experience taught her the importance of working together, and the importance of never giving up.

CHAPTER 2
CARE FOR WHAT YOU HAVE: A HUMBLE BEGINNING

Clara was raised in a modest four-room wood-frame farmhouse. The house lacked running water, electricity, and indoor plumbing. Meals were prepared on a wood-burning stove, and water was drawn from an outside well.

Growing up in a house without modern amenities, Clara learned to appreciate the value of simplicity and self-sufficiency.

She developed resourcefulness and a strong work ethic, as she had to actively participate in daily chores and find creative solutions to everyday challenges. This upbringing fostered her resilience and shaped her perspective on the importance of gratitude and the ability to thrive with limited resources.

The lack of modern conveniences significantly affected Clara's everyday life. The absence of running water meant fetching it from an outdoor well which was a time-consuming and physically strenuous task. Cooking on a wood-burning stove demanded continuous vigilance and exertion, making meal preparation a tedious chore.

Moreover, without electricity, they depended on daylight and alternative methods of warmth and illumination after dusk.

To stay warm during cold nights, they used a combination of blankets, layers of clothing, and a wood-burning stove, which not only provided heat for cooking, but also served as a source of warmth for the entire house.

This simplicity created a sense of tranquility and togetherness within the household, as the family gathered around the soft glow of the lamps, sharing stories and laughter.

In a world filled with constant distractions and busyness, Clara's tobacco farmhouse served as a sanctuary where the true essence of family and connection could be experienced and cherished.

WILLOW
SPRINGS

CHAPTER 3
CARE FOR YOUR COMMUNITY

Willow Springs was Clara's community, and it was a wonderful place where she grew up. Clara remembers feeling embraced by the familiar faces of the store clerks and how her father always took the time to explain the various products they encountered while shopping.

Taking trips into town not only gave Clara the opportunity to spend quality time with her father, but it also allowed her to develop a strong sense of belonging and connection within their community.

She hopes that future generations will also experience the same sense of belonging and community that she did, and that Willow Springs will continue to thrive as a haven of happiness and cherished memories for others.

The Leach family was well known and respected within the Willow Springs community for helping others as they were well known for their kindness and generosity. Despite having very little, they shared what they had with the less fortunate.

Their activities included assisting underprivileged families, offering free meals, and engaging in volunteer work. Furthermore, they participated in numerous local charities. The family continues to be a source of inspiration within the community, exemplifying the positive influence individuals and families can have.

They stood as paragons of kindness and compassion, serving as role models and demonstrating generosity's profound impact. The legacy they leave behind will endure through the various organizations and charities they support and motivate.

As a family, the Leaches were devoted to their faith, believed in prayer's power, and dedicated to serving others. In addition to generously sharing their time and resources, they consistently looked for opportunities to contribute to their community. Their kindness will ensure their legacy endures.

Chapter 4

Care for your Family: Clara's Parents

The love Clara had for her parents could not be denied! Being the daughter of Otha and Caretha Leach gave her immense pride. It was the dedication, work, sacrifice, and unwavering support they gave her throughout her life that she admired most.

Clara was proud of her parents and wanted to show love in return. She often helped her mother around the house and gave her gifts she made on special occasions.

She also supported her father in his work and was always there to listen to him. Clara was grateful for the life her parents had given her and was determined to repay them with love.

She worked hard to provide for them and was always there for them in times of need. She was grateful for their unconditional love and support and would never forget their influence in her life.

HOME
SWEET
HOME

CHAPTER 5

CARE FOR YOUR FAMILY: MOTHER

There was a warmth and nurturing quality found in Clara's mother, Caretha. Caretha had been a homemaker all her life and taught Clara how to cook. One of the greatest joys in Clara's life was spending time in the kitchen with her mother.

Clara was fascinated by her mother's cooking skills. She helped her in the kitchen and even learned how to make some of her famous recipes. Clara's dedication to learning her mother's recipes paid off, as she became adept at recreating her mother's famous dishes.

Whether it was a batch of warm, soft, melt-in-your mouth chocolate chip cookies or a tray of flaky biscuits, Caretha's baked goods always brought joy and satisfaction to her family and friends. Seeing her loved ones enjoy her cooking always made all the hard work in the kitchen worthwhile, Clara reflected.

Caretha's cooking skills became widely known amongst her family and friends as the best food in Willow Springs. She often received requests to prepare meals for special occasions. The joy Caretha felt when she saw the smiles on their faces light up the room, and the overflowing compliments she received for her delicious creations, made all the time and effort she put into cooking truly rewarding.

CHAPTER 6

CARE FOR YOUR FAMILY: FATHER

Otha's commitment to his work and livelihood was extraordinary. Despite the challenges associated with sharecropping and tobacco cultivation, he consistently faced his responsibilities with steadfast determination and discipline.

His example of hard work and persistence guided Clara and her siblings. His devotion to his family and strong work ethic motivated Clara to pursue excellence in her own endeavors.

She appreciated her father's guidance and support. Otha's unwavering dedication instilled a strong work ethic in Clara. This encouraged her to aim for excellence, fortified by the knowledge that diligence and perseverance will pave the way to achievement.

It was common knowledge within the family that Clara was her father's favorite child, something she took great pride in. Being her father's favorite child, Clara carried the weight of his expectations and held a special place in the family's dynamics.

This favoritism, while providing a sense of pride for Clara, also brought with it a great responsibility to live up to her father's high standards and maintain the family's reputation for kindness and generosity.

Clara learned the importance of discipline and hard work early in life and was able to apply that to her own life. She credits her father's legacy with many of her successes.

Throughout the summer, Clara enjoyed assisting her father in the garden, where they picked and cultivated vegetables for winter storage. It was a task she cherished. The hours they spent together were peaceful and calming.

Clara loved watching her father work, feeling the sun on her back, and breathing in the scent of the flowers. She was grateful for this time with him.

CHAPTER 7

CARE FOR NEW RESPONSIBILITY: DUTIES

At eight years old, Clara eagerly embraced her newly assigned farm responsibilities. Every morning, she rose early to feed the chickens, collect their eggs, and tend to the cows. Taking care of the animals became a cherished routine for Clara, deepening her connection with the farm and strengthening her bond with her father.

Clara enjoyed her time among the animals and came to appreciate nature's beauty. She also developed a deep appreciation for the effort required to manage a family farm. As time passed, Clara's respect for the land and its inhabitants grew profoundly.

She learned the importance of hard work and the satisfaction of a job well done. This experience taught her valuable lessons about perseverance and dedication, which she would never forget.

Clara's growing connection with the animals on the farm fostered a sense of empathy and understanding within her. She developed a profound appreciation for their unique personalities and the role they played in sustaining the farm. Clara found solace in their presence and recognized the reciprocal relationship between humans and animals, further deepening her love for the land and its inhabitants.

Otha always made sure to thank her for her hard work and dedication. Clara cherished these moments with her father and loved hearing the stories of the animals on the farm.

For Clara's help, her father would reward her on Sunday after church with a cone of vanilla ice cream, her favorite flavor.

CHAPTER 8

CARE FOR RESOURCEFULNESS: TEAMWORK

While Clara grew up without modern amenities, she learned to be resourceful and to work as a team. It was important to her that her family was self-sufficient, from the garments they made, to the vegetables they grew, and the meat they raised.

Clara's experience taught her the importance of working together and how to maximize limited resources. As a result of her experiences, she became inspired to teach others the skills she had acquired from living on her farm.

Clara's upbringing in a resource-limited environment instilled in her the values of resilience, self-sufficiency, and responsibility. These experiences shaped her belief in the power of hard work and the importance of taking care of your loved ones.

Clara and her siblings would often participate in competitions to see who could finish their chores the fastest, turning the mundane tasks into a playful and lively experience. Despite the demanding work, Clara cherished these moments of laughter and camaraderie with her siblings, creating unforgettable memories that would last a lifetime.

CHAPTER 9

CARE FOR HELPING: NEIGHBORS

Clara's sense of responsibility and willingness to help others extended beyond her immediate family. She often helped her elderly neighbors, assisting them with farm work, or other household tasks whenever the opportunity presented itself.

Clara's assistance had a profound impact on her neighbors' lives. Not only did she lighten their workload and provide them with much-needed support, but her encouragement to venture outdoors also improved their physical and mental well-being.

Clara's selflessness and compassion created a strong sense of community and uplifted those around her. She was always eager to teach them various coping skills and another way of doing things. She often shared her knowledge and wisdom with them, hoping to help them lead a more meaningful life. She also encouraged them to stay connected to their community.

She helped them prepare their grocery shopping list and joined them at the store. Additionally, she organized transportation for their doctors' appointments. She also assisted with meal preparations, made sure they had any needed medication and provided emotional support. She made it a point to stay in contact with her neighbors' family, keeping them informed about their well-being, all out of her deep care for them.

Chapter 10

Care for Joy: Playtime

Clara and her siblings often played outside when time permitted. The type of game played required them to fabricate their own homemade tools. Their jump rope was made from rope found on the farm, the hopscotch game was drawn on the ground with a stick, and Clara's favorite game was hide-and-go-seek.

Clara enjoyed playing games because it allowed her to explore her environment and interact with her siblings. Sibling interaction was crucial for Clara's development as it helped her build social skills, learn to share, cooperate, and navigate conflicts in a safe and familiar setting.

Another way Clara and her siblings would pass time would be going fishing down at the local pond. Clara's father did not care that much for fishing because of his duties that kept him busy, but Clara and her mother, Caretha, loved fishing. Clara and her mother would spend hours casting their lines into the serene waters, immersed in the natural world.

These fishing trips not only created lasting memories for Clara and her mother, but they also strengthened their bond and deepened their appreciation for nature.

Candlelight night games brought magic and enchantment to Clara and her siblings' nighttime routine. The flickering glow of the candles created a whimsical atmosphere, allowing them to escape into a world of fantasy and unlimited possibilities.

They loved to pretend to be princesses, fairies, and knights, engaging in imaginative play that brought them closer together. The atmosphere was peaceful and calming, and the glow of the candles was a reminder of the beauty of their time together.

The games created a sense of connection and companionship that Clara and her siblings would cherish for years to come. They shared stories and laughter and dreamed up wild adventures. The games gave them a sense of wonder and hope.

CHAPTER 11

CARE FOR YOUR SOUL: DREAMS

Clara's dreams were a driving force in her life that kept her going forward. She was determined to leave a positive impact and create a better future for herself and her family. However, Clara faced numerous obstacles along her journey. Financial constraints, limited access to quality education, and societal expectations were just a few of the challenges that threatened to hinder her progress. Despite these obstacles, Clara remained resilient and continued to push forward towards her goals.

Clara was destined to make an impact, whether through a career in law, medicine, education, or the arts. She was determined to use her talents to create a legacy that would live on long after her. She insisted on making a difference in the world. Clara refused to let anything stand in the way of her success.

Motivated to achieve her goals and make a difference, Clara was certain that her dreams would become reality through commitment and diligent work. Therefore, Clara remained steadfast in her resolve to create a legacy for generations to come.

PETER PAN
LITTLE WOMEN

Chapter 12

Care for Knowledge: Thirst for Learning

At the age of four, Clara was taught to read by her big sister. Being taught to read at such a young age allowed Clara to develop strong literacy skills early on, which would serve as a foundation for her education and future endeavors.

It also ignited her curiosity and love for learning, opening a world of knowledge and imagination that she would continue to explore. She quickly became obsessed with reading books and storytelling, and this passion has lasted throughout her life.

She found solace in the written world, as it allowed her to escape into different worlds and explore endless possibilities.

Through her love for reading and writing, Clara was able to express herself, unleash her creativity, and share her unique perspectives with others. It became her means of self-expression and a way to leave a lasting impact on the world. The books that she and her siblings read together at night continued to inspire her imagination, fueling her creativity, and shaping her into the storyteller she would become.

School Bus

Chapter 13

Care for New Experiences: First Bus Ride

Clara was one of those young girls who was extremely excited about attending school for the first time. Learning about new things was a dream come true for her.

She wanted to experience life outside the farm. Her opportunity was finally here, and she would take full advantage of it.

Before getting on the school bus, her mom would tell Clara and her siblings that it was their responsibility to pay attention in school and behave properly, however, if they did not obey, their evening would not be fun!

Clara's heart pounded with anticipation as she waited for her bus to arrive. As the bus finally pulled up, she eagerly climbed aboard and found the perfect seat next to her new classmates.

She could not believe how beautiful the countryside was as she watched the world go by through her bus window. She was excited to start this new chapter in her life.

Chapter 14

Care for Discipline: a Mother's Words

The reminder from her mom to remain responsible would silently echo in her mind as she observed the chaos around her and the lack of discipline from the other kids on the bus.

Taking a deep breath, she reminded herself that she was old enough to set an example. Mature enough to demonstrate proper behavior without escalation, she pulled out her notebook and pen, jotting down her objectives for the day.

She realized that her mother's words held a deeper meaning now, and she made a silent vow to maintain her focus and behavior despite the distractions around her.

Little did Clara know that this bus ride would be far from what she expected. The bumpy road, the loud chatter, and the uncomfortable seats quickly dampened her excitement, leaving her feeling disillusioned and longing for the familiar comfort of her home.

ABC
APPLE
BOAT
CA
SCIENCE
AND MATH FOR
CURIOUS KIDS

CHAPTER 15

CARE FOR OPPORTUNITIES: STANDING OUT

Clara's first experience in a classroom was incredible, and quite a contrast to her initial experience on the bus. While in the classroom, she was delighted to learn from her teachers and fellow classmates.

She was a perfect student and loved learning new things outside of her farm duties and responsibilities. As time went on, she realized that her discipline and rural upbringing had given her a unique perspective, and skillset that her classmates did not possess.

Clara shared her knowledge and experiences from the farm. She enriches classroom discussions and becomes a valued contributor to the learning environment. Her enthusiasm was contagious, and the students soon began sharing their own knowledge and experiences, creating a vibrant learning environment.

The teacher noticed Clara's dedication and appointed her as the class assistant. Clara was thrilled with her new role and continued to make a positive contribution to the classroom. Clara was an excellent student during her elementary school years. She was exceptional at learning and retaining what she was taught. In fact, Clara was such a natural and gifted student, that she was able to skip a few grades and start junior high school early.

This early advancement challenged Clara academically, enabling her to excel in her studies. She adapted to the advanced curriculum and established herself as a top student.

CHAPTER 16

CARE FOR EDUCATION: HIGHER STANDARDS

Clara's academic achievements brought her personal fulfillment and inspired her school-mates. She exemplified the transformative power of education and its potential to lead to excellence. Her example proved that with perseverance and commitment, any goal is attainable.

In addition to her academic achievements, Clara actively participated in various extra-curricular activities throughout high school. For example, she was a member of the debate team, where she honed her critical thinking and public speaking skills.

Her embodiment of excellence served as a beacon of motivation for all. Clara's example had a lasting impact on her classmates. She was a role model for those who wanted to excel and succeed in life. Her influence will continue to inspire generations to come.

Her achievements transcended societal expectations and broke through stereotypes, demonstrating that intelligence and determination know no limits. She was a symbol of strength and courage, and her story is a powerful reminder of what is possible. She demonstrated the importance of following your dreams and achieving success despite the odds. Clara remains an inspiration to us all.

Clara was also a member of the Science Club, where she further nurtured her passion for Science, Technology, Engineering, and Mathematics (STEM) subjects and conducted challenging experiments alongside her peers.

These activities not only enriched her high school experience, but also highlighted Clara's well-roundedness and dedication to personal growth.

The pride displayed by her parents contributed significantly to her self-esteem. Their recognition and validation of her accomplishments reinforced her sense of self-worth and instilled a strong belief in her abilities. This parental pride served as a powerful motivator, encouraging her to strive for excellence and pursue her goals with confidence.

Clara graduated high school at 16, she ranked second in her class and was honored with the prestigious Magna Cum Laude award—a remarkable achievement for a sharecropper's daughter.

CONGRATULA
MAGNA CUM LAU

NORTH CAROLINA AGRICULTURAL AND TECHNICAL
STATE UNIVERSITY
ARTS AND SCIENCES
1891
MENS ET MANUS
PUBLIC LIBRARY

Chapter 17

Care for Achieving Goals: College

Clara accepted the offer of admission to North Carolina Agricultural and Technical College (N.C. A&T) with great enthusiasm and pride. It was another dream come true. As she had a bright future ahead of her and understood how important it was for her to succeed.

Clara was determined to make the most of her college experience and embraced every opportunity for growth and learning that was ahead of her.

She knew that the challenges she faced and successes she had in college would lay a solid foundation for her future career and personal development.

Clara was fully committed to her academic success and understood that sacrifices would have to be made. She was willing to forgo late-night parties during the week to prioritize her studies and maintain high grades. During Clara's sophomore year in college, a classmate suggested that she pursue a career in nursing. She took the advice, and after a year, Clara was accepted into a nursing program.

Excited about the prospect of a new career path, Clara eagerly dove into her nursing studies. She found fulfillment in caring for others, and discovered a passion for the medical field that she never knew existed.

During her nursing program, Clara worked in a hospital and learned about patient care, which was challenging, but rewarding. Clara's experience in the hospital during her training allowed her to witness firsthand the impact she could have on patients' lives.

She saw the challenges of patient care, but also experienced the rewarding moments when she was able to be effective and provide comfort to those in need.

HEALTH
NURSING

LEACH

CHAPTER 18

CARE FOR ADVANCEMENT: HIGHER TRAINING

Through the supplementary nursing courses she undertook, Clara enhanced her expertise, refined her abilities, and demonstrated her commitment to service and excellence.

She finished the Advanced Pharmacology course, enhancing her knowledge of drug effects and interactions. She also completed the Critical Care Nursing course, which honed her skills in caring for critically ill patients. She then had the skills to provide safe, effective, and compassionate care. She was able to assess, diagnose, and implement treatment plans for a wide range of illnesses and conditions. She remains committed to continuing her education to stay up to date with the latest developments in healthcare.

Additionally, Clara pursued studies in Maternal-Child Health, Mental Health Nursing, and Geriatric Nursing, which expanded her scope of knowledge and equipped her to offer specialized care across diverse healthcare environments. She was considered the hardest working nurse in her class.

She is committed to providing the best possible care to her patients and works diligently to ensure that her team is always up to date and well trained. With her Bachelor of Science in nursing, Clara now has the academic foundation and credentials to support her extensive practical experience and leadership skills.

Clara is also highly organized and is always prepared to answer any medical questions her patients may have. She is also dedicated to staying up to date with the latest medical advances and best practices to ensure the best care for her patients.

YOU ARE NEEDED NOW
JOIN THE
ARMY NURSE CORPS
APPLY AT YOUR RED CROSS RECRUITING STATION

ANY SOLDIER
IS A GOOD SOLDIER!
THE WAC
WOMEN'S ARMY CORPS
Inquire at your local Army Recruiting Station or War Department Headquarters
ARMY OF THE CALIFORNIA REPUBLIC

Chapter 19

Care for your Future: the Army Nurse Corps

While walking to class one day, Clara noticed a sign stating, "The Army Corps Needs You!" This sign intrigued her for the rest of the day, and she could not sleep that night as her thoughts were consumed by the appealing prospect of joining the military. Compelled by this idea, she reached out to an Army recruiter the following day to inquire about becoming an Army officer.

The recruiter was impressed by Clara's enthusiasm and eagerness to join the Army. He invited her to visit his office to discuss her options further. Clara accepted the invitation and readily prepared for her visit.

Clara was excited and nervous at the same time. She knew her hard work and dedication had paid off and she was eager to take the next step in her career. She was confident that she had what it took to succeed in the Army.

PARENTAL
CONSENT
FORMS

CHAPTER 20
CARE FOR INDEPENDENCE: PARENTAL APPROVAL

Clara was uncertain how her parents would react, especially her father, as she considered joining the military.

Clara understood that her father had always dreamed of her pursuing her own career path, but she could not help but feel torn between her own aspirations and her desire to make her family proud.

Clara was still not of age to sign the paperwork to join the military, which required her parents to do so. After several talks and discussions with them, she was able to convince her parents to sign the paperwork that allowed her to join the military as an Army nurse.

Through their discussions with Clara, her parents recognized her passion for serving her country. They welcomed the idea of her joining the Army as a nurse and supported her dreams. It was important to them that Clara pursued her own ambitions, which also made them proud at the same time. In the end, it was a mutual agreement that benefited all of them. She signed the contract and immediately began to prepare for her military career. She was ready to take on the challenge of becoming an officer and to serve her country with pride. She was eager to begin her new journey and to make a difference.

I Serve..
ARMY

Chapter 21

Care for Serving: the United State Army

Joining the military not only fulfilled Clara's personal aspirations, but also provided her with a sense of purpose and fulfillment. She was immensely proud to serve her country and was committed to making a difference in the lives of her patients.

Clara was able to apply her nursing skills in a new setting while gaining valuable knowledge and experience. She was able to share her knowledge and skills with her fellow soldiers and civilians.

Throughout her service as an Army nurse, she was able to make a positive impact on the lives of others, contribute to her family's well-being, and broaden her horizons by experiencing diverse cultures and places.

She was also able to gain a keen sense of camaraderie with her colleagues, forming lifelong friendships. She found fulfillment in her career, knowing that she was making a difference in the lives of her patients. She ultimately found a sense of pride and purpose in her work.

LEACH
LONG

CHAPTER 22

CARE FOR MILITARY LIFE: A NEW BEGINNING

At the beginning of Clara's military career, she found it difficult to establish her niche in the vast world of the United States Army and often wondered if she had made the correct decision to join.

However, with the help of her colleagues, she realized her calling in the health care field was where she belonged. She embraced her role and made a meaningful impact.

Clara was proud of her accomplishments and the work she was doing. She was satisfied to find something that gave her a sense of meaning and purpose.

She eventually found a place where she could make a real and lasting impact, and that was through nursing. She had positive impacts on the lives of her peers, supervisors, and what she felt most important, her patients.

It was an honor for Clara to serve her country as she was grateful for the opportunity. Despite her initial reluctance, she eventually realized that she made the right choice by joining the military. As she observed the impact she was making on others, she felt a sense of purpose. The companionship and the sense of belonging that came with being part of something bigger than herself solidified her belief that joining the military was the best decision she ever made.

NURSING SKILLS
FUNDAMENTALS
CARETAKING
WOUNDS
EMERGENCIES
PATIENT CARE
ASSESSMENT
TRAUMA + PTSD
HYGIENE
LEACH

Chapter 23

Care for Teaching: First Assignment

During Clara's first assignment, she taught new nurses how to become better nurses, a trait that remained throughout her career. She believed that with the right guidance and support, anyone could achieve their goals.

She utilized her expertise to empower others, steering them towards becoming the best versions of themselves. She was passionate about seeing her peers succeed and she would often go above and beyond to help them achieve their own goals. She was also generous with her knowledge, often sharing her insights with those who needed it the most.

Clara's passion for teaching and dedication to helping others flourish continued to shape her career.

She became known as a highly regarded mentor and leader within the nursing field, who was always eager to share her knowledge and experiences with new nurses.

Her commitment to education and professional development makes her a highly respected figure in the healthcare community. She was an inspiration to all who knew her, and her legacy will live on through her former students and colleagues.

HOLY BIBLE

Chapter 24

Care for Promotion: General Officer

Over the next 34 plus years, Clara was promoted several times, eventually reaching the esteemed rank of Brigadier General. Clara would now be referred to as General Adams-Ender!

Her leadership skills and ability to inspire others were instrumental in driving positive change and improving patient care outcomes worldwide. General Adams-Ender's dedication to her profession and commitment to excellence continued to shine throughout her remarkable career.

She became the chief executive officer for 22,000 nurses, a director of personnel for the Army Surgeon General and she was the vice-president for nursing at the prestigious Walter Reed Army Medical Center.

She was the first African American woman to oversee a major military base – Fort Belvoir, located in Virginia, and the first female in the United States Army to be awarded the Expert Field Medical Badge (a special skill award in recognition of exceptional competence and outstanding performance by field medical personnel).

ARMY NURSE
N
CORPS
ADAMS-ENDER

CHAPTER 25

CARE FOR YOUR FUTURE: A LEGACY OF EXCELLENCE

After a successful military career, General Adams-Ender served in several key positions. She has received numerous awards and honors for her work and continues to be a strong advocate for veteran women. She continues to break down barriers for women in military and political leadership.

General Adams-Ender was a former Chair of the Andrews Federal Credit Union Board; a former member of the United States Marine Corps University Board of Visitors; and a former member of the Defense Advisory Committee on Women in the Services (DACOWITS); additionally, she served as the Chairman of the Board, The ROCKS INC, the only woman to serve twice in that position.

The ROCKS, Inc. association also provides career counseling, networking, and other support services for its members. The association's goal is to help young military officers and civilians to reach their potential.

She is currently the President and Chief Executive Officer (CEO) of Caring About People with Enthusiasm (CAPE) ...all because Clara Cares.

U.S. COMMAND AND GENERAL STAFF COLLEGE
LEAVEN WORTH
AD BELLUM PACE PARATI
FORT LEAVENWORTH, KANSAS

MARINE CORPS
UNIVERSITY

North Carolina
Agricultural and Technical
State University

THE ROCKS, INC.
Concern, Dedication, Professionalism

CAPE INCORPORATED

Andrews
FEDERAL CREDIT UNION

NATIONAL BAR
ASSOCIATION
EST. 1925

M
UNIVERSITY OF MINNESOTA
REGENTS OF THE UNIVERSITY OF MINNESOTA
OMNIBUS ARTIBUS

SCIENTIAE INTER ARMA SPIRITUS

ARMY NURSE
N
CORPS

NORTH CAROLINA AGRICULTURAL AND TECHNICAL
1891
ARTS AND SCIENCES
MENS ET MANUS
STATE UNIVERSITY

CHAPTER 26

AWARDS AND RECOGNITION

General Adams-Ender has been honored with numerous awards for her exceptional service in the United States Military and the civilian sector.

Her military honors include the Distinguished Service Medal with an Oak Leaf Cluster and the Regents. This is a military distinction awarded to soldiers for exceptionally meritorious service to the government in roles of significant responsibility. Additionally, she holds a Master of Military Art and Science degree from the Command and General Staff College in Fort Leavenworth, Kansas.

She has received many awards for her community work and service, including the Roy Wilkins Meritorious Service Award of the NAACP, Gertrude E. Rush Award for Leadership from the National Bar Association. General Adams-Ender was named the distinguished Graduate from the University of Minnesota where she earned a Master of Science in Nursing.

She has been awarded 15 honorary doctorate degrees in law, public service, humane letters, and science. In 1996, she was named by Working Woman magazine as one of 350 women who changed the world!

Chapter 27

Conclusion

Brigadier General (Ret.) Clara Adams-Ender lives life to the fullest from her residence in Lake Ridge, Virginia. In recognition of her contributions, Prince William County has named the street she lives on after her.

She finds joy in speaking with students, mentoring young adults, military members, nurses, and cherishing moments with her only child. She delights in recalling childhood memories with her siblings and exchanging life stories. These conversations foster a profound sense of connection and belonging. She is confident that regardless of life's journey, her family's support and love will remain constant. She values the relationships and memories she has created and is grateful for the warmth and comfort they bring. She carries them with her always, cherishing them like a precious gift.

ABOUT THE AUTHOR

Mr. Warren Edward Morris, the author of several children's books, is proud to share Clara Adams-Ender's story in his new publication Clara Cares. As a talented and prolific author in children's literature known for his captivating storytelling and ability to engage young readers, Mr. Morris has created a diverse collection of books that inspire the imagination and foster a love for reading. His latest work highlighting Clara Adams-Ender's remarkable journey is a testament to his dedication to crafting meaningful narratives that educate and empower children.

As a leader and motivator, Mr. Morris is passionate about helping others succeed. In his capacity as a humanitarian, he dedicates his life to serving others. A native of Prince William County, Virginia, Mr. Morris holds a Bachelor of Science in business management from the University of Upper Iowa. He has extensive expertise in counseling, marketing, and customer service. His career has been a great inspiration to children, who have learned to dream big and never give up from his meaningful role modelling efforts. He also supports programs and organizations that help children achieve their full potential while also advocating for their education.

Mr. Morris's consulting firm, With Essential Means, LLC (WEM), assists young individuals in comprehending the repercussions of their actions by guiding them in making positive choices and inspiring them to be exemplary role models for their peers.

Mr. Morris is writing his forthcoming book, "My Father, My Hero," due in late 2025. The narrative delves into the challenges a family faces due to a shift in their dynamics. It guides readers through an emotional journey, exploring the intense trauma experienced by the family and its impact on each individual. Moreover, the book sheds light on the family's fortitude and resilience, illustrating their collective efforts to overcome their struggles.

For more information about Morris's children's books and WEM,
visit **www.withessentialmeans.com.**